Basic Reading

BASIC READING

A. E. Tansley, B.Sc., M.Ed.

Manual for
Racing to Read
Early to Read
Sound Sense
Listening to Sounds

Best wishes

[signature]

E J ARNOLD & SON LIMITED LEEDS

0 560 00501 6

First edition   1972
Second impression   1973

Published and Printed in Great Britain by
E. J. ARNOLD & SON LIMITED LEEDS

Contents

This manual is intended to be a guide for teachers to the best ways of using the reading schemes in which the author has been involved. These series, which form a comprehensive reading scheme when used together, have been published by E. J. Arnold & Son Limited, Leeds, under the following titles:—

Racing to Read

A series of 12 books designed to teach a basic sight vocabulary of 200 specially chosen words. It can be used as a beginning scheme for *all* Infants.
6 recorded Packettes or Cassettes cover the contents of books 1–3.
A workbook accompanies these recordings.
A second workbook is available, covering the contents of books 3–6.

Early to Read

A series designed parallel to *Racing to Read*. The vocabulary is slightly different, the repetition and vocabulary load are less rigidly controlled, and three workbooks are included, one being a perceptual training programme.

Sound Sense

A series of 8 books adopting a new approach to the teaching of phonics.

Sound Sense Extension Books

8 books to review the work of the first three books in the *Sound Sense* scheme.

Listening to Sounds

A recorded programme of 36 twenty-minute lessons, (available on 9 Packettes, 9 Cassettes, or on 9 open spool tapes,) designed to give training in various aspects of auditory perception and phonics; there are two workbooks and the tapes also include work with the *Sound Sense* books.

Authors of reading schemes are naturally prone to claim that their work will guarantee success, particularly if it is based on some novel approach which they claim to have pioneered.

The history of the teaching of reading abounds with claims for numerous methods and techniques, but many such claims have not stood the test of time. No such claim is made for the schemes mentioned above. However, it can be stated, that they are the result of vast experience, particularly in connection with helping slow learners and children with acute reading difficulties. They have been thoroughly evaluated and incorporate improvements based on the author's research and experiment over a period of some twenty years. The continuing popularity of the earliest books *Sound Sense* and *Racing to Read* is perhaps a testimonial for their educational worth.

This manual, which is not intended to be a book on the teaching of reading, sets out to show teachers the educational and psychological principles upon which the total scheme is based. It will include suggestions about making the best of the methods and techniques involved and about adaptations to meet the needs of individual children.

1 Basic Principles in Teaching Reading

In writing the series of books included in the total reading
programme, certain basic ideas were used to inform the work.
The results of research, experiment and experience have in
recent years led to some changes in ideas and emphasis.
One of these has been concerned with the hastening of
reading readiness. The earlier ideas about learning readiness
were based on theories related to concepts influenced
by intelligence testing, which led to beliefs that readiness
was largely a matter of maturation and could be directly
related to mental ages. Teachers therefore had to wait
patiently for signs of readiness to manifest themselves. These
concepts have not been accepted in the production of the
scheme. They have been replaced by the theory that global
estimates of ability, for example, as expressed in test ages for
mental ability, language development, perceptual
development, and motor proficiency, are of little educational
use in that they give no indications to teachers about
teaching methods and programmes. These global estimates
should be replaced by more detailed studies of the specific
skills involved in a field of learning and the sequences
through which these skills develop. It is also postulated that
the acquisition of these skills can be accelerated to a degree
by appropriate programmes of training.
A further change is that if the various skills involved in an
area of learning, such as reading, can be isolated, it becomes
possible to arrive at a more efficient diagnosis and assessment
of a child's degree of readiness. This diagnosis can be made
much earlier than previously, and effective learning
programmes can be devised. An important by-product of this
kind of approach is that a more scientific and comprehensive
attack on learning readiness is possible and this often means
that children are protected from learning tasks for which they
are not ready in one area of development or another.
This deeper investigation of skills and learning processes is
leading to changes in ideas about the organisation of play and
in attitudes about the use of the 'play-way'. It is gradually
dawning on teachers of young children particularly, that

placing children in a "good nursery environment", or in what
is subsumed under the description of "stimulating
environment", does not guarantee success with some children.
Of course, play in all its forms is vital, but the need for the
integrated, programmed development of skills, (motor,
language and so on), is now being more widely accepted.
This principle has formed the base upon which *Early to Read
Book 1* and the recordings for *Listening to Sounds* and
Racing to Read have been constructed.

The basic principles used in the scheme are as follows:—

1   **Each child is a unique individual** responding to the
    environment in his own individual way, and maturing
    uniquely. This implies that the method used to teach a child
    to read should be more or less specific to him. There cannot
    be, therefore, one method of teaching reading which is
    universally applicable.

2   **Reading involves a number of skills** which develop at
    different times and at differing rates. These skills, which are
    open to training, are mainly concerned with visual and
    auditory perception which are the summation and
    interpretation of sensations principally acquired during the
    sensori-motor stage of growth. There appears to be a clear
    association between visual and auditory perception and motor
    and language development.
    There is still much to be learned about the way the skills
    develop, but it is generally agreed that visual perception is
    usually in advance of auditory perception in pre-school
    children and the younger infant in school. In other words,
    young children seem to be visually ready for reading before
    they are auditorily ready. This is probably due to
    environmental conditions in which greater attention is given
    to visual stimulation. Thus in reading readiness programmes,
    there has in the past been a greater emphasis on the visual
    skills than on auditory ones. They include assessment and
    training in hand-eye co-ordination, visual discrimination and
    matching, copying, classifying and remembering shapes, and
    visual short-term memory. Even in recent years, some
    perceptual training programmes were at first solely concerned
    with visual perception and included training in auditory
    perception in later revisions.
    It is contended here that, although there may be some
    substance in the theory that children's visual processes mature

somewhat in advance of auditory ones, the development of auditory perception skills can be accelerated by providing the right experience and suitable training. The *Listening to Sounds* recordings are an attempt to demonstrate what these experiences should include and the form the training should take. Experience with the taped lessons certainly appears to substantiate the thesis that acquisition of the auditory perception skills assumed to be involved in reading can be hastened.

It could be, therefore, that the methods used in teaching the beginnings of reading could be influenced by this claim so that phonics could be introduced much earlier than is at present assumed. Fifteen years ago, when I was working under the influence of traditional psychology (although intellectually I had begun to reject aspects of it), I concluded that the vast majority of children should be taught the beginnings of reading by a whole-word-sentence method. Early work on phonic readiness*, had, at the time, appeared to demonstrate that a child needed a word recognition reading age of $6\frac{1}{2}$ years before phonic readiness was achieved. The *Racing to Read* books were written with this objective, arrived at empirically by observing the responses of backward readers, in mind.

Later work with children suffering from acute reading failure has necessitated a revision of the above evidence. An analysis of the perceptual problems of the large group of children concerned clearly indicated that they had many difficulties in visual perception, but more especially in auditory perception. These auditory problems included difficulties in sound discrimination and sound blending, but particularly marked were difficulties in auditory sequencing (related to poorly developed short-term auditory memory), and auditory rhythm. It was the encouraging response of children to the auditory training in parts of a comprehensive perceptual training programme which led to the conclusion that all children could benefit from such training. Teachers using the *Listening to Sounds* recordings and the auditory rhythm exercises in *Early to Read Book 1 (Getting Ready)*, will be able to evaluate the validity of the claim.

The present position therefore is that it is perhaps still advisable for the majority of children to start reading by a

*Bragg, H. 1962 *Readiness for Phonics in Dull Children, Special Education,* Vol. L1 No. 2.

visuo-motor, visuo-spatial approach, i.e. the acquisition of a specially selected sight vocabulary. However, they should at the same time have programmed training in auditory perception and rhythm with a view to as early an introduction of phonics as possible.

3   **There are many ways in which children can be motivated to read.** In the past, the predominant one was *interest*. Books were judged by the interest level of the language used and the illustrations as related to the text. It seemed, and to some reviewers of books it still seems, that if children could be interested in a book, they would not only want to read it, but would be able to read it. It is probable that this narrow concept of motivation has created a substantial number of backward, frustrated readers. It was based on the middle-class experiences of teachers and authors who were dealing mainly with children who had a stimulating pre-school environment resulting in good language development, wide interests and some reading ability already acquired. Experience with children slow to read, led to a different understanding of motivation. They want not only initial success, but *continuing feelings of success*. This is also true for all children, but particularly for the majority of children who do not enter schools well-prepared for learning, yet with high expectations by themselves and their parents. It is very necessary, therefore, to introduce reading in such a way that success will be achieved and *maintained*. The interest motive is, of course, important, but the predominant one seems to be *mastery*. If this is so, it becomes necessary to write books for children with sufficient control of vocabulary load and repetition that continuing feelings of mastery are obtained. This may mean that the *interest* factor has to take a subordinate role. Children beginning to read want to *read* to obtain recognition and please teachers and parents. In these early stages they appear to be more interested in the process of reading than in what they are reading about. In any event, the children's language development and range of interests are bound initially to be far ahead of the content of first readers. With growing mastery, content becomes more and more important. Early books should, therefore, be related to interest as much as possible and to language and thinking development, but mastery of the process of reading should be the primary aim in the early stages. The *Racing to Read* and

Early to Read books are an attempt to achieve this difficult compromise.

4 **Reading is part of the total process of communication**
which involves the receptive and expressive aspects of
language, speech, writing as a means of expression, and
gesture. Reading is not, therefore, solely concerned with the
decoding and encoding of visual and auditory stimuli. It has
eventually to aid the acquisition of concepts and
comprehension and in so doing assist the development of
language. However, reading development is also assisted by
language, and books designed to teach the beginnings of
reading must be based on this mutual relationship. In other
words, it is desirable that the first reading book should be
built round the child's language in order that mechanical
reading should not be emphasised to the detriment of reading
with and for comprehension. One reason for the move away
from a phonic approach to the beginnings of reading was a
realisation that the phonically regular words which had to be
used were often unrelated to the children's vocabulary levels
and their use necessitated linguistic forms not used by
children in their everyday language. When this was also
supported by research findings in the 1920's and 1930's
which indicated that for most children a mental age of seven
was necessary for phonic readiness to be achieved, the
abandonment of phonic methods became almost complete.
Recently, the importance of phonics in the teaching of
reading has been re-emphasised and various techniques have
been introduced (or perhaps re-introduced in a different
guise) to meet claims for their outstanding efficacy.
This reading scheme is based on the thesis that most children
need to be *taught* phonics at some stage in their learning to
read. The timing of the introduction of phonics will be
discussed later. However, the importance of phonic reading is
mentioned here because of its relationship to language
development. If reading development is to keep pace with
spoken language development, the use of phonics is
essential to improve the children's word recognition skills.
The *Sound Sense* books represent a new approach to the
teaching of phonics in that they make use of language
development to help phonic teaching, and vice versa. They
are not an English scheme, but can be used as such for slow
learners. Teachers will know of many children who eventually
become so proficient in reading as a result of developing

phonic ability that they are able to read material which they cannot comprehend. *Sound Sense Book 8* takes this into account in suggesting ways of using good reading ability to improve language usage.

5   **A reading programme has to have breadth as well as length.** No reading scheme is sufficient of itself. A well-organised programme of supplementary reading is an integral part of a school's reading scheme. However, a successful beginning to reading for many children needs control of vocabulary load and repetition. The use of too many books, at first, which use widely differing vocabularies can be confusing and even frustrating to children who find reading difficult. The contention here is that for children wanting a whole-word-sentence approach, the vocabulary load and control of repetition in the *Early to Read* and *Racing to Read* books is such that they require no supplementary books to establish mastery of the beginnings of reading. If teachers find that supplementary material is desired, it should normally be made by them and be related to the specially selected vocabulary of the books. This can be done by preparing workbooks, writing additional material using the given vocabulary, preparing work-cards and comprehension exercises and, as some teachers have done, writing simple plays about the stories used in the books, e.g. 'Lost in the Cave', for children to read and act. If the use of other books is considered to be necessary, they should be chosen with great care.

As the child's reading ability grows, and he is able to use word recognition skills effectively, the use of supplementary reading for interest, information and story content, should be gradually extended. Thus, as the child works through the *Sound Sense* books, increasing use should be made of supplementary reading, if only to demonstrate to the child the expanding usefulness of his growing reading skill. The supplementary reading should, of course, be related to the child's reading levels in mechanical reading, speed of reading, and comprehension.

6   A good reading scheme should consist of related parts:—
a) A comprehensive programme of reading readiness activities and training, which includes receptive and expressive language stimulation, play, sensori-motor development, the acquisition of perceptual skills, and

attention to emotional and social factors. It is important to emphasise that children achieve readiness in these areas at differing rates, and even in an individual child developments may be uneven. Children can, of course, often make a satisfactory start in reading without reaching a given level of development in all areas. However, as will be seen later, in motor, sensory, and perceptual development it now seems that definitive levels of development or achievement are needed if a successful beginning is to be made. These levels also appear to indicate which reading method is likely to be appropriate at certain times in the acquisition of reading skills.

Further aspects of the concept of learning readiness are important. In the case of reading, it is wrong to imagine that readiness is an all or none matter. As I have pointed out, "readiness is itself a developing, dynamic process".*
Children are always 'getting ready' for higher levels of learning. This is obviously one of the prime considerations in programmed learning. In the teaching of reading, for example, phonic readiness has to be systematically developed from the simplest levels of auditory discrimination and perception and auditory memory to more advanced levels involving speedy auditory sequencing, auditory closure and blending, and syllabication.

As stated earlier, readiness can be hastened by supplementary play with structured programmes of training in particular skills and perhaps in language. This is particularly true for children who have suffered deprivation in sensori-motor and language growth as has been demonstrated by work done with children in Educational Priority Areas.

b) The acquisition of word recognition skills by visual and auditory means. Reading is basically a visual and auditory process and the sooner the two processes can be involved the quicker will progress be. It must obviously be wrong to concentrate almost entirely on one sense modality to the exclusion of the other. Thus, if the development of a basic sight vocabulary is considered appropriate initially, teaching to develop and make use of the auditory channel must be used simultaneously. Conversely, a phonic beginning must be accompanied by the use of visual cues. Indeed,

*Tansley, A. E. 1967 *Reading and Remedial Reading,* London: Routledge and Kegan Paul.

modern theories of learning, such as that suggested by Hebb*, indicate that efficient learning has a motor basis and also requires a multi-sensory approach to ensure maximum cortical stimulation.

c) The development of speedy relaxed reading for information, ideas and pleasure. It seems that controlled and systematic teaching of reading has to be continued until reading ages for word-recognition, speed and comprehension have reached something like a nine-year level. Thereafter, for most children, opportunities to use reading in stories, widening interests and subject areas, are all that is required to maintain progress. Nevertheless, with children slow to learn, even these opportunities need careful planning if frustration caused by difficulties is not to result in diminished motivation and even retrogression.

d) At the highest level of reading development, the skill should be employed to assist the growth of creative thought, and concise, logical communication. The present scheme does not, of course, purport to teach reading to this level of competence. However, teachers can anticipate this level by taking every opportunity to encourage children to discuss word meanings and content and thereby enrich the ideas and concepts acquired from reading.

*Hebb, D. O.   1949   *The Organisation of Behaviour,* New York: John Wiley.

2 Reading Readiness Programme

The importance of reading readiness has already been mentioned and I have written at length elsewhere about it*. It is perhaps sufficient here to mention that a comprehensive scheme for hastening readiness must include inter-dependent and inter-related programmes for:—

1 **Motor development** to the stage where the child has good posture, smooth well-co-ordinated gross and fine movements, good body awareness, and unilateral dominance of hand and foot. Physical education which encourages the achievement of this stage is thus a most important part of the readiness programme.

2 **Sensory channel and sensory integration development.** Children need experiences to develop the efficient use of all the sensory channels — vision, hearing, touch, smell, taste, and movement appreciation (kinaesthesis). However, recent work with children with acute reading problems has demonstrated that although the individual sense modalities, particularly the visual, auditory, tactile and kinaesthetic, are important, it is sensory channel integration that is essential. A child may have no problems in seeing and in visual perception (i.e. in interpreting what is seen), and in hearing, but if he is unable to integrate visual and auditory stimuli he *will not be able to make a start in reading*. In the *Listening to Sounds* tapes, lesson one is designed to diagnose any difficulty in visual/auditory integration and to suggest ways of training this.
Again, if a child cannot explore an object by touch and identify it on visual presentation or by naming (provided it is known to him), difficulties in beginning to read are most likely. Further, if a child is given a movement, or kinaesthetic, imput (by holding his hand and drawing a figure or shape in the air without his seeing it) and cannot identify the figure

*Tansley, A. E. 1970 *Reading Readiness* (Ed. M. Chazan) University College of Swansea.

or shape from a visual display, he is unlikely to be able to read. Teachers will be able to discover the other sensory channel integrations involved. They should all be investigated as part of normal class method and, where necessary, training programmes which use language as much as possible should be devised and applied regularly and systematically. Auditory-motor integration is of unique importance in phonic readiness and will be mentioned later in connection with the perceptual training programme.

3   **Perceptual development** with particular reference to visual and auditory perception. Children reared in stimulating homes where a wise selection of toys, games and general activities is used will have adequate opportunities to develop sensori-motor abilities and perceptual skills. Some children, however, who are deprived of these opportunities, or because of abnormal neurological development, and other conditions, are unable to acquire perceptual skills without help. Such children, if denied this help, are very likely to experience great difficulties in starting to read. For them, a systematic programme of perceptual training to supplement the more usual activities at the pre-school and early school stages is absolutely necessary. Research work in Birmingham is demonstrating that some 25 per cent of 6–7 year olds have learning difficulties of a perceptual nature which interfere with learning the basic subjects. It is essential that teachers should be aware of this and be capable of organising activities and training to overcome the problems and to prevent increasing backwardness and associated emotional disturbance.
It should not be thought, however, that training in perception is needed only by children who are slow to learn or deviant in some way. It is suggested that *all* children will benefit from such training, particularly between the ages of four to seven years. It is further posited that this training will hasten the development of perception to a point of reading readiness, and make it possible for children to read much earlier than has hitherto been thought likely.
The reading scheme therefore begins with the perceptual training programme given in *Early to Read, Book 1*. The exercises in this book have been used in the author's previous school for some ten years and are now being used widely in many schools in this country and abroad. The exercises, which are briefly described below, are also of diagnostic use.

It has been found that children not capable of coping with most of the visual perception work — in particular copying figures and shapes, discriminating visually, and hand-eye co-ordination work — are usually not ready for a whole-word-sentence approach. Children unable to do the sound rhythm exercises, that is saying, tapping, and saying and tapping simultaneously the suggested rhythms or sequences, are *nearly always* unable to tackle a phonic approach.

Before briefly describing the different exercises it should be emphasised that they must be supplemented by activities and games which will assist the programme. For example, while perceptual training is being used, the motor development programme should be used as well; games designed to give practice in hand-eye co-ordination, matching pictures, visual discrimination, auditory training in sound pitch, intensity, timbre and rhythm, visual and auditory memory, and the naming, classification and drawing of shapes and patterns should be used extensively but in ways programmed to the child's level of development. It should be further stressed that the various exercises should be used together; that is, training in all areas of perception should go on contemporaneously. Even when a child has successfully made a start in reading, the perceptual training programme should be completed. It is particularly important for teachers to note that if a child makes a successful visual start, training in auditory perception along the lines given in the early recorded lessons of *Listening to Sounds* is essential to prepare for phonic readiness, and indeed to hasten it.

The nine perceptual training areas are as follows:

1   **Hand-eye co-ordination.** All these exercises should be preceded by the use of toys and blackboard work using grosser movements to give practice at an easier level. The book exercises themselves have been carefully programmed to provide additional practice in getting hand-movement and eye-movement working smoothly together and to develop within the child a sense of direction from left to right and up and down. Continuous movement should be encouraged until the individual task has been completed; poor performance can often be improved by encouraging the child to "talk to his hand," e.g. by saying "steady, steady", or "side, side, stop, down, down, stop". It may, of course, be necessary at first

to hold the child's hand and guide it; the degree of such help should be gradually reduced.

In order to provide adequate practice on each individual task, it is useful to cover the page with an acetate sheet and use a chinagraph pencil or felt pen.

The exercises are arranged in order of difficulty, but for some children the insertion of additional exercises may be necessary. The programme might well be extended to give controlled practice in the early stages of formal writing.

2 **Copying stick figures** to give training in visual copying and form perception. The child should be given spent matches and asked to copy the figures but not by placing the matches on the book figure. When difficulty is experienced the task should be discussed — which way is the match pointing?; are the two matches touching?; is the match head pointing towards you (downwards) or away from you (upwards)? In cases of extreme difficulty the child should be encouraged to feel the matches as he talks.

It is often advisable to give the child one shape at a time to copy, and for younger children and those with lack of fine muscle control, the matches should be replaced by large blocks of wood or sticks. Some teachers doing this training with groups have found the use of an overhead projector very beneficial. The teacher makes the figure or pattern on the projector, talks about it, and then asks the children to reproduce it.

To aid form perception and visual memory, the child should be asked to reproduce the figures from memory, first using matchsticks or larger sticks and later as a pencil and paper task. Further supplementary training in form perception should include the following:

a) The classification and naming of shapes including circles, squares, oblongs, triangles, diamonds, trapeziums, etc. More difficult classificatory exercises should deal with variations in size, colour and texture; shapes on shapes, or shapes with other shapes cut out, combinations of shapes.

b) The construction of three-dimensional models from two-dimensional representations using individual blocks or shapes.

c) A variety of carefully programmed jig-saws starting with puzzles based on the human figure. The simplest of these will be two-piece in which the child has to put top and bottom together, and this will lead to three and four-piece puzzles with horizontal cuts. Vertically and obliquely cut figures then follow and finally the more usual jig-saw of increasing complexity. These puzzles of the human figure are useful in helping the development of body awareness which is so important as the foundation of all learning.

d) Perceptuo-motor tasks such as copying shapes. To hasten development of this, much use should be made of tracing round templates, making Aloplast or clay shapes, finger painting and simple appliqué and collage work. Again the overhead projector can be very useful in motivating and improving these types of perceptual task.

It has been found over a number of years that *copying the match stick figures given in Early to Read Book 1 is a very useful readiness test for predicting ability to cope with a sight vocabulary approach to reading.* Experience has given unequivocal proof that children unable to cope with the shapes cannot learn a sight vocabulary. It has also tended to show that training in this exercise hastens readiness.

Similarly it has been found that *children unable to copy satisfactorily the figures below are very unlikely to make progress* using a visually orientated method.

Training in copying these figures along the lines indicated appears to be a fundamental part of any perceptual training programme.

3   **Training in visual discrimination and orientation** to improve laterality and refinement of discriminatory processes. The *matching cards* in *Early to Read* are used for this training and instructions are given in Book 1 of the series. Again, experience has shown that the programming of the individual exercises is about right for most children. However, teachers may wish to increase the number of tasks to make the programming less steep. They may also wish to reproduce a form of the programme using larger figures and shapes. It will be noted that some of the eighteen tasks in Exercise C, Early to Read Book 1 involve size discrimination.

As in the case of the match stick figure work, children having great difficulty should be encouraged to use language to aid discrimination, and feeling the drawings will help. It is important that children should eventually be able to do the exercises correctly in order to obviate reversals and inversions in later stages of reading, writing and spelling. Since laterality is involved, the connection between these exercises and the motor development programme will be obvious to teachers. The use of visually presented patterns for children to step out has been found useful as a visuo-motor integration task which improves discrimination. The children are given graded cards such as the one below, and they walk and talk the exercise.

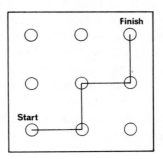

These discrimination exercises are also a good guide to visual perception readiness.

4   **Copying figures and patterns** according to the given instructions and then reproducing them from memory. This is another perceptuo-motor task but is also useful in training visual memory.

5   **Training in remembering visual sequences.** For those teachers and psychologists familiar with the Illinois Test of Psycholinguistic Abilities, test profiles reveal that a common weakness in slow readers is failure in visual and auditory short-term memory and sequencing. Exercises to train these have, therefore, been included in the *Early to Read* perceptual training programme. The instructions in the book give a clear indication of how visual sequencing may be trained. Creative teachers will be able to devise games and other tasks to supplement the recommended exercises. In training, naming the sequences will be an aid to visual memory development.

6   Training in figure closure and completion. Again the instructions are explicit. The suggested training should be augmented by the addition of more figures and shapes, by asking children to say what is happening in a picture in which only part of the action is visible, and by the use of pictures with 'hidden' drawings of animals, objects, etc. e.g. how many animals can you find in this picture?

7   Training in temporal sequencing. The 'making the story' exercise is designed to train children in placing events in temporal order. When a child is reading, part of the total skill concerns the remembering of letters or phonemes in time order as well as visual and auditory sequencing. Teachers will have met children who are capable of remembering the individual letter sounds which have to be blended to make a word but who cannot remember the sounds in temporal order (e.g. which sound is first or last) when attempts at blending are made. Again teachers who work with children suffering from language disorder e.g. dysphasia, will know of children who fail to say words in the right order to make good syntax. It is very likely that part of the reason for this is a disturbance in temporal sequencing. Thus, although the degree of the significance of temporal sequencing in the reading process is not known, it does seem that the skill is necessary.

The "stories" in *Early to Read* consist of only four pictured events. Teachers should make their own card material to give more extended stories of up to ten events. It is very important to remember to get the child to tell the story when the picture sequencing has been completed. It is also educationally valuable to remove the sequenced pictures and ask the child to repeat the story from memory.

8   Training in visual sequencing. Exercise H entitled *Sight Patterns* is designed to test and train the child's ability to appreciate visual rhythmic sequences as a part of visuo-motor training. Thirteen rhythms are given but teachers may well wish to include more. During training sessions, the child should be encouraged to say the rhythms as he points to the example and continues drawing the pattern. This will provide further training in visual/motor/auditory association.

9 **Training in auditory sequencing and rhythm.** The pictures used in the picture sequencing exercises mentioned in 5 may also be used in assessing and training auditory memory and sequencing. For example, place the picture of the window, tree, chimney and apple in front of the child and ask him to pick up the ones named in the order in which the names are given. More pictures may be added to extend the range of difficulty. Then replace the pictures (or actual objects if working with younger or retarded older children) by the geometrical shapes and repeat the form of training. Experience has now shown that a child's ability to deal with sound patterns and rhythms is of extreme importance in readiness for reading, and particularly for phonics. Exercise I in *Early to Read Book 1* is therefore very significant. The evidence is so strong that it is possible to state that if a child cannot say the given rhythms and tap them after demonstration by the teacher he will not be able to listen to letter sounds, remember them in sound and time order, and blend them into words. In other words, he will not have success with phonics.

More recent work has shown one further aspect of this training which is of even greater significance. It was discovered that some children could say and tap the rhythms quite adequately, but could still not blend sounds together, although the indications were that short-term auditory memory was not significantly poor and no detectable hearing loss even for higher frequencies was found. Further investigations revealed that these children were unable to say and tap the rhythms simultaneously. In other words, their auditory-motor association process was defective — they could not 'talk to their hand' and make it respond in co-ordination with language. I believe this inability is of paramount importance in explaining the failure of some children, often intelligent and occasionally described as dyslexic, to cope with the analysis and synthesis of sounds. Training in auditory-motor integration is therefore an essential part of any reading readiness programme. In addition to the work suggested in 'Getting Ready', training should include the following:

a) More difficult rhythms than the ones given.

b) Writing the rhythms using a dash, dot pattern. The child should try to write and say the rhythms simultaneously. The ability to do this is not a *sine qua non* of phonic readiness and work with nursery school children has revealed that it is difficult for most four and some five-year olds. It is therefore more useful in helping older reading failures.

c) Learning and saying jingles and nursery rhymes.

d) Singing and moving to action songs.

e) Walking, running, hopping, skipping and dancing to simple rhythms.

f) Conducting an imaginary orchestra.

g) Talking to parts of the body and moving the parts according to self-given instructions, e.g. right hand up, down, up, down, etc, etc.

h) Scribbling or finger painting to tapped rhythms or music with a strong beat.

i) Listening to and obeying commands.

The first two *Listening to Sounds* tapes give examples of how auditory memory, auditory sequencing and rhythm may be trained and should be used as an integral part of the readiness programme.

There can be little doubt that any reading readiness programme should include the described perceptual training programme,* or one similar in structure and programming. It is essential for children who appear to be experiencing difficulty in starting to read or who have made a start but fail to maintain satisfactory progress.

*To be published shortly.
The Tansley-Davies Perceptual Training Programme which is based on the programme described in this chapter.

3 Beginning to Read

The child's response to the readiness programme described in Chapter 2 will, of course, be a good guide to his readiness to begin reading. However, other aspects of readiness should not be minimised. The level of the child's language development and his ability to communicate will be important. His general attitude to learning as demonstrated in his ability to attend and concentrate, his eagerness to discover things for himself, his willingness to work and co-operate with other children and adults, and the desire to read that he displays will obviously all have significance to the teaching situation. The general class atmosphere is of fundamental importance in stimulating a keenness to read and must be based on good teacher/child relationships which give the child security through understanding, a sense of belonging through friendly encouragement and acceptance, and feelings of successful achievement through well-planned, individualised programmes of instruction.

Building a Sight Vocabulary

If the child's profile of readiness activities reveals that a sight approach should be used, it is necessary to ensure that reasonable effort on his part will lead to early feelings of achievement. It is essential, therefore, that teachers prepare him for the day when he will be introduced to his first book. The visual perception part of the readiness programme will have been extended into such activities as picture matching, word-to-picture matching, and word-to-word matching using words which will be met in the first reader, e.g. *Racing to Read, Book 1, My House, My Garden.* A series of lottoes based on the *Racing to Read* and *Early to Read* books will also help teachers and children in this type of activity. Furthermore, the teacher should encourage language and activities which will arouse and enrich the child's interest in the reading content of the first book. In *Reading and Remedial Reading* (op. cit.) I have described in some detail how some teachers have planned activites to ensure that the child will be introduced to the first reading book with a reasonable chance of initial success.

The busy teacher of infants, however, will find it difficult to organise and carry out these activities with large groups of children at varying levels of readiness and reading ability. To help in this situation, six Packettes comprising 24 taped lessons of approximately twenty minutes duration each have been recorded. They are to be used in conjunction with the *Racing to Read Workbook*. Briefly, these tapes contain much pre-reading book language work and a variety of activities and exercises to help the child acquire the sight vocabulary used in the first two *Racing to Read* books. The recorded lessons will give indications of how to prepare children for meeting the later books in the series and in the *Early to Read* books. The latter include two workbooks which have been devised to further this type of preparation and provide consolidation.

Experience shows that after the early books have been completed the control of vocabulary load and repetition is such as to obviate a continuance of comprehensive preparatory work. Some picture- and word-matching work or writing and tracing words for which pictures are drawn by the children themselves may remain necessary, particularly for slow learners. Moyle* gives examples of exercises he devised as a remedial teacher to ensure continuing success with the *Racing to Read* books, but he also says that after extensive use of the series he has discovered 'the repetition to be adequate even for very dull children to memorize the vocabulary and yet not lose interest in the story'. He stresses, however, the necessity 'to point out letter discrimination in order that the pairs of words *green* and *garden, wall* and *window* are not confused'. This emphasises the need for adequate preparation by the use of exercises similar to those on the *Racing to Read* tapes.

The vocabulary content of *Racing to Read* is 200 specially selected words with an additional 109 words, which consist of compounded words, e.g. *seaside, greenhouse*, plurals, participles and inflexions. The first 125 words were chosen from an analysis of words used by children in talking about their interests, the most frequently occurring words being used in the published schemes. This vocabulary was supplemented by an additional 75 words chosen from other language studies. The average repetition of the 200 words throughout

*Moyle, D. 1968 *The Teaching of Reading*, London: Ward Lock Educational.

the 12 books in the series is 109, the more commonly occurring words being repeated to the point of *overlearning* to make their recall automatic.

The vocabulary in the four readers of *Early to Read* consists of 80 words of which 74 are common to *Racing to Read* but repetition is less. These books may, therefore, be used as first readers for brighter children or as supplementary reading when the early books of *Racing to Read* have been completed.

Many teachers have produced their own material for *Racing to Read* including flashcards, comprehension exercises, word games, and workbooks. The two workbooks included in the *Early to Read* series have been designed to be used in conjunction with *Racing to Read*.

Experienced teachers who have used the *Racing to Read* books over many years, have reported one very interesting observation, namely, that when children have been adequately prepared for beginning Book 1 they all make extremely parallel progress through the remaining books. This has applied to even dull children. This observation would appear to suggest that the programming of the books is at a near optimum level for ensuring steady, continuous progress. However, if this progress using a sight approach is to be maintained at later stages, it is vital that the development of phonic readiness should receive attention during the period of acquiring the 200 sight words.

During the early experimental work with the *Racing to Read* scheme the teachers were asked not to use any incidental work in phonics. If a child did not know a word he was simply told it and it was studied by prescribed work in his individual workbook. However, work on letter sounds, e.g. listening to sounds at the beginning and ending of words, matching letter sounds to their symbols, was undertaken when children appeared to be ready for this type of activity. A good guide to this readiness was the child's ability to say how words were alike. For instance, each child had an alphabetically indexed book in which words he knew by sight were written by the teacher or copied by the child. If, for instance, the child could discern the point of likeness in *ball, big, by, boy,* he was showing clearly that he was associating the initial letter with a sound and was therefore ready for studying letter symbol and sound associations. To further this, much classification work was organised. The child was given an envelope or plastic packet of pictures. He had to put pictures in sets according to initial or final letter sounds, the appropriate letters being given for the sounds used. For example, an envelope might include pictures of a c<u>ar</u>, c<u>aravan</u>, c<u>at</u>, c<u>aterpillar</u>, <u>b</u>oy, <u>b</u>aby, <u>b</u>ottle and <u>b</u>at and two cards one with 'b' and another with 'c' on them. Variations on this were 'Letter Bingo' and 'I spy', which most teachers now use, and also work on rhymes and jingles.

This earlier work tended to be rather unsystematic and experience demonstrated that there was need for a thoroughly programmed approach to preparing children for the use of phonics in developing word recognition skills. Such a programme should teach children to listen to sounds and associate them with printed symbols, to write letters for sounds, to practise auditory rhythms, to develop short-term auditory memory and sequencing, and eventually to blend sounds together into phonograms and words. Furthermore, the programme should take into consideration the relative difficulties in learning individual sounds and blends, the frequencies of sounds used particularly in reading schemes, the need for a multi-sensory approach, and the apparently wide variations in the speed with which children acquire phonic ability. It also seemed necessary, for many children, to present the early stages of auditory discrimination and perception work in good quality sound reproduction and in relation to phonetics, i.e. the correct reproduction of letter sounds.

My experience has tended to show that phonics are generally badly taught because teachers seem to have no real training in this area of teaching reading. I have attempted to demonstrate how I believe this pre-phonic and phonic work should be tackled by recording the *Listening to Sounds* tapes and devising the two *Listening to Sounds* workbooks. The first two tapes include work on auditory-visual association, auditory memory, listening, rhymes, and auditory rhythm and auditory-motor association. The next three tapes include exercises to teach the sounds for <u>t, n, s, p, g, ing, d, m, l, f, b, r, c, h</u>, and <u>w</u>. Where possible, the sound of a letter is taught as it occurs at the *end* of words, when its sound is more strictly phonetic and pure. For example, the sound for the letter <u>t</u> is first introduced as it is heard at the end of the words <u>foot</u>, <u>hat</u>, <u>bat</u>, <u>boat</u>, <u>net</u>, <u>cot</u>, <u>dart</u>, <u>nut</u> and <u>tent</u>. Next it is taught as an initial sound.

A multi-sensory approach is ensured by visual and auditory association and by the saying-writing method where appropriate.

The evaluatory work with the tapes and workbooks appeared to demonstrate quite clearly that the programming is good for children as young as three and four years of age, and also for older children with reading difficulties. Children in special schools with acute learning difficulties, and even those with emotional problems have responded most encouragingly to the material.

The recorded material is a boon to teachers in helping them to organise their class work to meet a wide range of reading abilities. Children can work either individually or in groups (a junction box and pairs of stethoscopic headsets are useful for groups) with little supervision and without disturbing the rest of the class or having themselves to contend with distracting classroom activities.

As stated earlier, it is confidently asserted that the use of the recorded material supplemented by much classificatory and oral work and games will hasten phonic readiness and permit a quicker association of sight and auditory attacks on reading. Indeed, for some, probably brighter children with good language development, a mixed-method approach is possible from the very beginning. The pre-phonic work of the tapes can be sufficient for these children to make use of auditory clues in an incidental way and with a minimum of help, and their reading ages improve so dramatically as to make nonsense of standardized reading tests. The problem with some of these children is to ensure that comprehension keeps pace with mechanical reading.

4 The Teaching of Phonics

Some reference has already been made to certain aspects of phonic readiness in connection with the development of auditory perception and discrimination. The importance of auditory rhythm and sequencing, and of auditory-motor integration in programmes for hastening phonic readiness has been stressed and indications have been given of how a child's response to auditory rhythm activities may be used as a pointer to phonic readiness. There are, however, other abilities which appear to be involved and which need to be developed to certain levels before children may safely be introduced to phonic programmes. These abilities appear to be:—

1 **An ability to appreciate rhymes:** for instance, picking out the non-rhyming word in a set of otherwise rhyming words; supplying from a given choice of words, or spontaneously, a word which rhymes with a given word or set of rhyming words; using the game 'I Spy' to find an object or action in a picture whose name rhymes with a given word.

2 **An ability to discriminate between letter sounds.**
These exercises are very useful:
Which of these words is out of place or is a stranger —
Man, met, mill, cap? (beginning sounds)
Which of these words is a stranger —
cat, hat, foot, hit, fire? (ending sounds)
Which of these words is a stranger —
pot, cap, hop, box, lock? (middle sounds)

Listen to these words — baby, boat, boy, box.
Which of these sounds do they start with — c, p, b, t?
Listen to these words — cot, bat, tent, sit.
What sound is at the end of all of them?
Tell me a word which begins with 'f' (giving the correct phonetic sound, not the alphabetic name) as in the game 'I Spy'. As a variation, the teacher may use the child's sight vocabulary and ask him to choose words which begin or end with a given phonetic sound.

3 **An ability to blend sounds.** This, as most teachers will realise, is of fundamental importance in using phonics and has to be developed and tested with discretion. The child who is unable to blend sounds together is unable to make satisfactory progress. Teachers are well aware of the dangers in blending — for instance, "cu-a-tu" does not blend into "cat". In such instances, it seems preferable to use initial sounds — "ca-t, bi-g" — after the children have been taught the blending of sounds which can be blended smoothly, e.g. m-a-n, s-i-t, l-e-g.
In the actual teaching of phonics to most children, not too much emphasis should be placed on blending because this can lead to an exaggerated analytical approach and a reduction in reading speed by making it difficult for the children to read without paying too much attention to detail. One way of avoiding this atomistic approach is to encourage children to find sound pronunciation, or meaning units within words, although, here again, there are obvious dangers, e.g. car in the word caravan. The teacher should aim at a happy compromise between a sight and phonic approach and should always bear in mind the use of contextual clues and comprehension.
A further method of developing the child's ability to use phonic analysis is to make use of sound likenesses in words. For example, if the child knows the word "and", he can soon learn sand, land, band etc; if he knows the word "sit" he easily learns sits, sitting and can move to fit, fits, fitting, hit, hits, hitting. This combination of phonic analysis and what is called structural analysis is given in considerable detail by Gray* and is worthy of serious consideration, particularly by teachers of slow learners.

4 **An ability to associate auditory sounds and visual symbols.** Exercises containing the following instructions are useful:
Put a ring round the letter for this sound.
Write the letter for this sound.
Write the letter that these words begin with.
The training of all these abilities is included in the *Listening to Sounds* scheme and the use of the tapes will certainly help teachers to organise the work of individual children or groups. Very careful consideration has been given to the programming of this training, and experience has shown that children
*Gray, W. S. 1948 *On their own in Reading,* London: Ginn.

(including older children with reading problems) enjoy doing the exercises involved and often make quite remarkable progress. This training is certainly an integral part of the phonic readiness programme.

Testing Phonic Readiness

The child's reaction to the early tapes of *Listening to Sounds* and his spontaneous efforts to use, say, initial sounds in attacking unknown words will constitute a superficial assessment of his readiness for more formal teaching of phonics. However, it is useful to be able to be more objective in an assessment of readiness and to diagnose specific weakness in any of the abilities described previously. This is particularly useful in a clinical situation or in making decisions about a child's level of phonic skill. A phonic readiness test may therefore be a useful instrument for teachers to have at their disposal. Such a test based on assessing the abilities, has been devised by Bragg and its use is described in *Reading and Remedial Reading* (op. cit. pp. 40–44). The correlations given should now be viewed with caution, because at the time the research was carried out a systematic programme for developing and hastening phonic readiness was not in use.

The beginnings of phonic teaching

Some general principles to be borne in mind when introducing phonics are given in *Reading and Remedial Reading* and it is not necessary to repeat them all here. However, some of the more important ones are worth reiterating.

These are:—

1 Reading in general, and phonic knowledge in particular, should be treated and taught as part of language development. Oral work, writing and spelling should be included in a phonic programme.

2 New letter sounds and phonograms should be introduced in words which are known by sight (if a sight method has previously predominated) or in words included in sentences which help the child to make intelligent guesses from context clues. From these words the child may be asked or helped to make a generalisation about the phonogram's sound. The generalisation should then be applied to words which can

reasonably be expected to have occurred in the child's spoken but not reading vocabulary. The application should be consolidated by a variety of exercises. The new learning must then be immediately integrated into 'reading for meaning' by using it in passages to be read and understood. Thus the functional use of new learning is demonstrated at once and helps the child to appreciate the usefulness of his new skill.

3   Drill and practice are essential if learning phonic skills is to reach a stage of being almost automatic. However, the drill must be seen to be purposeful and serve as revision and consolidation of work previously completed. It must also be presented in such a way that interest and motivation are maintained. To achieve this and provide the necessary amount of revision and repetition, drill and practice must be used in a variety of ways.

4   New learning must be presented not only logically but in relation to the psychological development of children. In deciding the content and ordering of it in a phonic pro-gramme, a compromise has to be reached between the frequency with which sounds occur in language and the difficulty experienced by the children in learning the sounds. For example, in teaching the five short vowel sounds, it is necessary to know the frequency with which they occur in words in common usage, and also the relative difficulty with which children learn their individual sounds and the use of these in phonic reading. Little research has been done on these aspects of phonic teaching, but the programming of the *Sound Sense* books, which have been used now by many teachers over a number of years, has not been criticised.

The eight *Sound Sense* books were written with the intention of meeting the demands made in (3) and (4) above. Thus, drill, repetition and revision were ensured by using a variety of exercises and activities. These include:—
Putting words into families according to given criteria.
Spontaneous giving of words which belong to a given family.
Finding strangers in lists of words.
Putting in missing sounds.
Rearranging jumbled words into sentences.
Word puzzles and crosswords.
Choosing the right word from alternatives.

Completing sentences.
Word sums and puzzles.
Finding rhyming words.
Classification exercises.
Giving or matching opposites.
Writing stories when key words are given.
Finding single words for phrases or definitions.
Changing tenses.

In an attempt to meet the two criteria of frequency in language and difficulty in learning, the sounds are introduced in the following order, with frequent revision:

Book 1 — a e i o u
Book 2 — ee oo
Book 3 — long a i o with final e
Book 4 — ar er or all
Book 5 — sh st th (2 sounds) ch
Book 6 — wh bl tr dr fr gr fl cl. Final y (as in <u>fly</u> and <u>baby</u>)
ea (as in <u>tea</u> and <u>dead</u>)
Book 7 — ai ay, oi oy, ou ow (2 sounds), oa, au aw.
Book 8 — igh, er ur ir, ew, ge dge, air are, ie, (2 sounds)
-tion -ation -ection, sion, ph, kn, gn, wr,
hard and soft c

This order is not necessarily an optimum one but many years of experience of testing the reading ability of children who have used the whole scheme systematically shows that from a reading age of 6–6½ for Book 1, reading improved comparatively evenly to an average reading age of 10½ years when Book 8 had been completed. Even with slow learners, many of whom were maladjusted and neurologically abnormal, there have been consistent gains of 10–11 months of mechanical reading age per year during a period of some fifteen years, for the early part of which the scheme was used in cyclostyled form. For brighter children, particularly when well-organised supplementary reading is used (see later), much larger yearly increments of reading age have been very common.

5   For satisfactory learning to take place, careful attention must be given to motivation. The teacher's relationship with her class and its individual members, her attitudes and the emotional tone she develops, are, of course, vital in the development and maintenance of enthusiasm, keenness and satisfactory work habits. Nevertheless, she needs the support of well-graded learning situations. In *Sound Sense*, therefore, special attention has been paid to the grading of exercises and the frequency of revision in order to ensure that the child's feelings of success are cumulative. The phonic check list in Sound Sense Book 1 is intended as a simple diagnostic test of phonic skill, but should be used principally to decide at what stage individual children should begin the scheme. Checks carried out each term will be an indication of the quality of learning and progress. However no books can ensure continuing success for all children; the grading of exercises can at best be such that it satisfies the needs of the majority. In using this phonic scheme, therefore, the teacher must keep in mind the individual differences in her class. For some children, the grading will be too easy. In such cases some of the consolidation exercises might be omitted. For others, the grading, particularly in the later stages, may prove to be too steep. For these, additional oral and written exercises, and perhaps teacher-made card material and games will be needed.

Since it has been proved by experience with the books that the early stages of the programme are so important to lay firm foundations for later progress, the *Sound Sense Extension* books have been produced. They are basically readers which use a vocabulary to give further actual practice in reading to revise and consolidate the work done in the first four books of the series. A few additional exercises are included for those children who might benefit from them. One further reason for producing the extension books was to provide a *controlled* application of the learning achieved in the first books and to allow the child to realise success in using his new learning.

There are some children who, quite early on, acquire a special ability in analysing and blending sounds and are able to read almost any phonically regular words. Such children may well have a mechanical reading age much in advance of comprehension. The obvious treatment in such cases is to provide plenty of exercises which test understanding of reading content. It may be as well to point out here that although the use of writing and written exercises should be encouraged as an aid to reading, their use can be over-emphasised with certain children. For example, I have come across children who, because of poor fine motor-co-ordination, find writing difficult, and because of too great an insistence by teachers on written responses, have been held back in developing phonic skills. One experience in a school for physically handicapped children will demonstrate the point. A child was working on *Sound Sense Book* 3 and with great effort and concentration – he was an athetoid – was writing the answers to the exercises. I asked him to tell me the answers rather than continue to write them. He could do this without any difficulty. I then gave him exercises from later books in the series and he had little difficulty with exercises in Book 7. He was, therefore, learning nothing about phonics and, if it were necessary to train writing skills, could have been working at a much higher comprehension and interest level. In other words, he was not being sufficiently motivated in the total learning situation the teacher had planned for him. In using the *Sound Sense* books for their primary purpose, this boy should have been allowed to tell the teacher the answers or better still, to record them on a tape recorder for later checking by the teacher. Since he had a slight speech defect too, the use of the tape recorder would have been doubly beneficial. Many handicapped children remain underfunctioning because of failure on the part of teachers to adapt their methods and techniques to the children's individual learning needs.

The wise teacher will use the *Sound Sense* books, as indeed she will use any of the total scheme and other aids, in such a way that none of the children become frustrated and antagonistic because the work is too difficult, or bored, apathetic and restless because it is too easy.

6 Research into phonics, particularly in this country, has been mainly conspicuous by its absence. What research has been done has produced equivocal results varying from claims for complete victories for phonic approaches over 'look and say', to absolute defeat. It is probably true that children taught by good, convinced teachers obtain good results whether or not they are taught phonics. Bad teaching always begets bad results.

However, the research findings and experience appear to show that phonic instruction in some form or other is necessary for most children at some stage in their learning to read. It is not essential to every child because some brighter children, or those with unusual auditory skills, are able to make their own phonic generalisations and apply them to unfamiliar words, particularly if they are encouraged to use contextual clues. Incidental help is all that such children require. For the vast majority, and certainly for slow learners, *systematic instruction in phonic skills is essential* and produces far better reading results than incidental instruction, particularly when what is taught is transferred immediately to reading situations. It is almost certain that reactions against the use of phonics, particularly in the past, were largely due to their introduction before readiness had been achieved, incidental instead of systematic teaching, and poor programming and presentation of instruction and materials. The *Sound Sense* books represent an attempt to overcome these shortcomings of teaching.

Further Suggestions to Teachers

1 For most children, the *Sound Sense* books are not designed to teach the beginnings of reading. They are most useful for children who have acquired a sight vocabulary and have had systematic training in the various aspects of auditory perception and phonetics which have been mentioned. They have been geared to the *Racing to Read* series but can, of course, be used in conjunction with any reading scheme. They have been found to be useful for children who appear to use a phonic approach from the beginning if used in conjunction with a phonically based early reading scheme like the *Royal Road* series*. Indeed, one of the authors of the *Royal Road* books has recommended the use of the *Sound Sense* books as consolidating or, in some instances, preparatory material.

2 Any new word containing phonic elements, which the child has not studied should normally be treated as a sight word. This is important in the early stages for all children, and particularly so for backward readers. However, if children have worked through the early tapes of *Listening to Sounds*, it is desirable that the knowledge of letter sounds acquired should be used in reducing a completely 'trial and error' attack on words. After all, the reason for teaching phonics is to aid word recognition to reach the stage, as quickly as possible, when phonic analysis is so quick and automatic that reading by sight is achieved.

*Daniels, J. C. and Diack, H. 1956 *Royal Road Readers,* London: Chatto and Windus.

3   Since in his early reading the child's attention, in the majority of cases, has been focused on visual similarities and differences in words, and the connection between these and sounds has been incidental, it is important that when he starts using *Listening to Sounds* and *Sound Sense* his attention should be drawn to sounds and sound families. The recorded lessons should achieve this, but when the child starts studying word families in *Sound Sense Book* 1 it is possible for him to give correct answers by visual inspection rather than sound similarity or association. For example, cat, fat and mat will be put together correctly as a family not because they have the same vowel sound, but because they all contain the shape a in the middle. Oral practice is therefore very essential at this level. The association between sight and sound should be emphasised. However, the teacher should not over-emphasise the association by saying, for example, that a always makes the same sound as a in the word apple. This only leads to confusion later and to the development of faulty reading habits.

This stage of teaching phonics, when the child is studying the sounds of the short vowels and begins to make use of blending, is perhaps the most important and yet the most difficult to teach. Many children continue to have reading problems until the difficulty has been removed. In order to help teachers, I have recorded how I have taught children at this level. The later taped lessons are largely based on *Sound Sense Books* 1 *and* 2 and it is hoped that the method used will prove helpful to teachers and avoid problems for the children. Recordings have not been made for later books in the series, because it is felt that when children have completed the nine cassettes or tapes they will be sufficiently sophisticated to continue making steady progress by using the *Sound Sense* scheme alone.

4   Some phonic elements are known to present more difficulty than others, although there are wide differences in individual children. These differences are often due to variations in children's hearing ability and level of auditory discrimination. For instance, children with even slight high frequency deafness have difficulty in hearing high frequency sounds like *s, sh, ch, z*. Other difficulties may be due to area differences in the production of individual sounds as part of dialect. Teachers should bear these difficulties in mind,

because they may require particular treatment by using additional written or tape-recorded material.

5   Previous references have been made to the great importance of blending sounds into words and the dangers inherent in its teaching. Apparent inability to blend is frequently experienced with backward children and unless great care is exercised in developing readiness and correct presentation this can result in faulty reading habits and unfavourable attitudes. The following hints, some of which have been mentioned earlier and have been given in more detail in *Reading and Remedial Reading* (op. cit.) are useful in these cases:

a) Make sure the child can say, tap, say and tap the rhythms in *Early to Read Book 1.*

b) Make sure the child can blend individual sounds orally before presenting the visual symbols to him. Correct phonetic pronunciation should be used. The *Listening to Sounds* tapes include this work.

c) Pay particular attention to final and initial sounds and to the sequence of sounds in spoken words.

d) Give training in auditory memory as suggested earlier.

e) Where possible, emphasise the use of writing and saying the word as a unit, or combination of smaller units. For children with great difficulties, finger tracing of the word as it is spoken is a great help. When using this procedure great care should be taken to ensure that the child does not pronounce the word letter by letter as he writes or traces. Smooth blending must be encouraged. For example, if the child is learning the word sheep he should say sheep slowly as he writes or traces, not shu-ee-pu.

6   Do not use the books in such a way that all the class are working on the same exercise. Class teaching should now surely be anathema to all teachers. Every child should be allowed to go ahead at his own pace provided his previous work has been thoroughly mastered. He should be competing against himself. In any class there may well be children working on each of the eight books in the scheme. Usually,

the more efficient the teaching the greater will be the spread of attainment.

7 While the *Sound Sense* books are being used as the basis of the phonic programme, a rich variety of supplementary activities should be provided.

a) Supplementary Reading

The *Sound Sense* scheme is not designed to teach reading. Its sole purpose is to teach the application of phonic analysis and synthesis to the development of speedy word recognition. The method used which involves language development and oral and written work is suggested as a new approach.

Children learn to read by reading appropriately organised material. A wide variety of books covering a range of reading ages should be used to give practice and consolidation of the phonic skills being taught. Each child's supplementary reading should be just below his reading age to ensure that his incidental reading is successful, meaningful and, therefore, pleasurable.

Hundreds of children using the scheme have been given yearly word recognition tests and it is, therefore, possible to say, with reasonable accuracy, what reading ages are achieved at different stages. The following table is given as a good guide.

Sound Sense Books	Supplementary Reading Age
1	6 –7 years
2 and 3	7 –7$\frac{1}{2}$ years
4 and 5	7$\frac{1}{2}$–8$\frac{1}{2}$ years
6 and 7	8$\frac{1}{2}$–9$\frac{1}{2}$ years
8	9$\frac{1}{2}$–10+ years

It will be noted that there is a steady progression through the scheme. Experience shows that the best results have been achieved by teachers who have best organised the supplementary reading. More information about ways of selecting supplementaries is given in *Reading and Remedial Reading* (op. cit. pp. 52–54).

b) Supplementary Writing

Free writing should be encouraged throughout. The more ways in which the children can apply new learning the better. Exercises in more directed written expression should also be included as in formal comprehension work, the giving of clear, succinct descriptions or definitions, letter writing, sending telegrams, and factual reports of events. As will be seen later, it is recommended that formal spelling should be taught when phonic teaching begins. It is worth stressing therefore, at this point that when marking the children's free writing work only those spelling mistakes which should not have been made at the child's level of spelling attainment should be corrected. Nothing is more depressing to children than pages of work full of teacher's corrections.

c) Supplementary Listening
Children need to have stories or verse read to them. Developing the art of listening plays an important role in developing phonic ability.

d) Supplementary Oral Work
Again encouraging a child to talk, recite and discuss is also likely to lead to improvements in phonics. Teachers should set good examples of well-modulated and clearly enunciated speech for children to imitate, and should encourage clarity of speech in the children. Dramatic activities, choral verse speaking, and singing are all valuable supplementary activities.

5 The Teaching of Spelling

The formal teaching of spelling has of late received less attention than formerly because of the 'modern' method of using what is called 'free expression' or 'creative' approach to the teaching of English. However, it is suggested here that the systematic teaching of spelling should be an integral part of the teaching of reading, and particularly phonics, both being important elements in the development of communication skills. There seems to be ample evidence in practice to support the view that the teaching of spelling supports the development of phonic ability and word recognition. In the light of this evidence it is recommended that formal teaching of spelling should begin at the time the children are ready to begin work on *Sound Sense Book* 1. Prior to this, during the time when the majority of children are acquiring a basic sight vocabulary, spelling should not normally be taught in a systematic way. As indicated earlier, during the pre-phonic stage children should be encouraged to write words they are learning by sight. The *Racing to Read* tapes, for instance, make much use of writing in copying words and even in encouraging attempts at writing words from memory. The early *Listening to Sounds* tapes attempt to teach children how to recognise the commonly used consonantal sounds and how to write their letter equivalents. This use of writing during the early stages of learning to read plays a vital part in the multi-sensory method which is recommended. It should not, of course, be stressed to such a degree that it inhibits 'sight' reading; it is of particular value to older children with reading difficulties.

There are, of course, inherent difficulties in teaching spelling in its supportive role to reading development. If the method used is over-analytical, it may well lead to an over-analytical approach in reading and inhibit the attainment of speedy sight reading in which phonic knowledge reduces trial and error attempts and limits the possibility of error. Again, teachers may decide to link spelling and reading so closely that reading development is held back by specific difficulties in spelling; this might well happen in neurologically abnormal children who have fine motor-co-ordination difficulties or visuo-motor association problems of a specific type. Yet again, auditory-motor problems may be such that while phonic blending is possible in the purely reading situation they interfere seriously with spelling development. Nevertheless, it is probably generally accepted that the spelling and writing of sounds and words being learned in reading, together with their use in sentences, is an important aid to mechanical reading and comprehension.

One further point must be made before definite suggestions are given about the organisation of a systematic programme for teaching spelling. Any class, no matter how homogeneous its composition may be thought to be, will have a wide range of spelling ability and attainment. Class teaching is therefore very ineffective; individual or group teaching must be used. In classes of younger children, the range of attainment may be from children who are not ready for formal spelling, or have specific difficulty, to children with spelling ages far in advance of their chronological age. The class organisation should be such as to meet the needs of all its individual members. If classes are smaller the children may be able to work in pairs; it should be possible in any circumstances to organise in groups of not more than six children. The groups will be comprised of children with roughly the same spelling age, although it is often useful to have one child of good spelling ability and attainment as leader or 'teacher'. It is always good social training for the better children to be given opportunities to help weaker ones.

Suggestions for organising the teaching of spelling

1   Group the children in as small groups as possible according to spelling age. This may mean that at the beginning of a year or term the class should be given a standardised spelling test. However, teachers using the total reading programme described in this manual will be able to group children according to the stages they have reached in the scheme.

2   Use the assignment technique in which children work through assignments at their own rate. The 110 assignments given later have been used to good effect for many years. The first assignment is for children with spelling ages of about 5 years or, better still, for children who are working on *Sound Sense Book 1*.

3 Each group of children is given the appropriate assignment for the particular group. The teacher (or group leader) ensures that the children pronounce each word correctly.

4 The individual words of the assignment are then copied into the child's spelling book and the teacher ensures that the copy is correct.

5 The children, preferably working in pairs, now study each word in the following way:

a) Each child looks at a word, tries to memorize it and then write it from memory. One child may then ask the other to write the word, and then be asked in turn. The written word is immediately checked with the correct copy. This procedure is repeated until the children (either each pair or the whole group) can spell all the words in the assignment correctly. Many children find it helpful to say the word slowly and smoothly as they write it.
Oral recall is not allowed or encouraged because spelling should be mainly a visual/kinaesthetic operation if it is to be speedy and, as here, enhance the development of reading by sight. It is important, therefore, that when asked to spell the word, the children should *write* it. Saying at the same time brings in the auditory aspect of the operation.

b) When the children feel able to spell all the words in the assignment, they ask the teacher or leader to test them. They are asked to write all, or selected, words from the particular assignment.

c) The teacher then asks the children to write sentences of their own which include words from the assignment, or gives previously prepared exercises which involve writing the words. Oral sentences may be accepted, particularly where it is considered that the children know how to incorporate the words in communication and might be frustrated by too rigid an adherence to written exercises.

d) Nevertheless, it is important to ensure that spelling is taught as a part of general language development and not as a splinter activity.

e) When the children have successfully achieved the previous study, they are moved on to the next assignment. Some simple form of reward for completing each assignment is desirable, particularly for young children and slower learners.

f) The assignments should be used imaginatively. For some children, it will not be necessary for all the assignments to be used. For others, additional assignments may have to be compiled and more frequent repetition and revision be used. Experience has shown that spelling taught systematically and regularly by this method and organisation results in spelling ages keeping more or less in line with reading ages. Large discrepancies are rare and when they do occur indicate the need for diagnosis of specific weaknesses (say in auditory–motor association, temporal sequencing, poor writing ability related to poor co-ordination of fine motor activity) and a more prescriptive approach in teaching.

Suggested Spelling Assignments

These are suggested assignments to be used in conjunction with the *Sound Sense* series. The words used are, with very few exceptions, taken from the *Sound Sense* vocabulary. The assignments are arranged in the order in which the words occur in the eight books. Thus, assignments 1 to 15 cover books one and two; assignment 61 coincides with the introduction of the phonogram 'ea', and so on.

The assignments are not necessarily arranged according to difficulty of spelling. Teachers may therefore wish to experiment with the order and make modifications in the light of experience.

Words which are phonically irregular have been included at appropriate levels and provision has been made for repetition and revision. Here again, however, modifications for individual children may be necessary.

Assignment 1
am   an   at   as   cat   ran
man   and   the   pass

Assignment 2
fat   hat   bag   bad   can
cap   had   has   we   be
me

Assignment 3
big   in   is   it   if   him
his   kill   kiss   no   so   go

Assignment 4
bill   bit   did   fill   fit   hill
will   miss   one   six

Assignment 5
on   of   off   not   box
dog   God   got   boss
hot   lot   job

Assignment 6
hut   cup   cut   run   fun
bun   you   are   but   girl

Assignment 7
get   ten   egg   red   men
met   bell   fell   less   read
with

Assignment 8
leg   let   wet   net   bed
full   pull   bull   draw
words

Assignment 9 Revision
am   fat   big   kill   dog
hut   get   leg   bell   pull

Assignment 10 Revision
we   no   one   boy   girl
read   draw   words   with
go   be

Assignment 11
cool   noon   roof   soon
tool   food   moon   too
room root

Assignment 12
foot   wood   wool   took
look   book   cook   good
poor   two   page

Assignment 13
tree   sheep   bee   week
need   deep   feed   seed
feel   keep   see   three
four

Assignment 14
seen sweet been feet
meet seem green seek
here said was

Assignment 15 Revision
egg roof food wood
cook week keep poor
two page four

Assignment 16
cake game late name
same came gate ate
do love

Assignment 17
race lace face lake
make take save gave
wave dear come made

Assignment 18
like time side ride
hide wide mile mine
line nine five today

Assignment 19
fire ice nice wife
white tire size black
blue seven eight

Assignment 20
rose hope home hole
rope bone nose June
Sunday Friday

Assignment 21
racing making saving
facing taking waving
hiding icing riding
hoping coming

Assignment 22
name love race make
dear come made like
side nine

Assignment 23 Revision
today fire white blue
eight hope rope making
waving facing

Assignment 24 Revision
one draw get book
here said

Assignment 25
car far farm park hard
mark dark yard party
Monday Spring many

Assignment 26
garden market farmyard
all ball wall hall tall
call fall small well
she or

Assignment 27
her after letter under
over better sister
summer butter baker
however teacher

Assignment 28
dinner driver finger
farmer matter ever
never clever number
paper river winter

Assignment 29
silver supper cover
answer wonder yesterday
September October
November December

Assignment 30
caller taller smaller
darker every give gone
happy have help street
left

Assignment 31 Revision
park market many small
summer teacher clever
driver answer wonder

Assignment 32
for nor corn torn
horn worn thorn horse
morning fort lord sort
any

Assignment 33
story forget north
doctor more before
begun begin ago alone

Assignment 34
sheep shall sleep shop
shed shut shape shake
shine shaking shining
smoking does

Assignment 35
fish bush cash dash
dish rush wish shopping
shutting shipping dashing
wishing rushing shooting
shilling

Assignment 36
would should could
wash school water yes
step still stop

Assignment 37
star stove stand start
storm stamp stone
stood understand some

Assignment 38
best dust fast just last
lost must nest past
cost rest west test

Assignment 39
most post carpet
shopkeeper who what
also hand eye finish
use near

Assignment 40. Revision
morning any doctor
shake shopping should
waterfall understood
postman some stamp
who shining

Assignment 41
thank think thing the
than they this that
something sometimes

Assignment 42
mother father brother
other another gather
fourth fifth sixth
seventh tenth together

Assignment 43
month though although
through thought there
these nothing those

Assignment 44
almost afternoon anything
your aunt uncle woman
open

Assignment 45
church chest cheese
choose child children
chase chime choke
charm chap across

Assignment 46
much such march ditch
fetch match pitch
witch stitch catch
patch watch inch

Assignment 47 Revision
something another fourth
although there thought
anything aunt woman
watch match

Assignment 48
why when where wheel
which whisper while
friend suppose pretty

Assignment 49
blot bless block blade
bleed blind blossom
able table stable
thimble tumble bubble

Assignment 50
dress draw drive drink
drop day drill drove
drip ladies song

Assignment 51
old cold hold told
sold gold talk walk
once sell sick milk

Assignment 52
from fruit freeze frozen
free frill frost frock
none people suit

Assignment 53. Revision
where table pretty
drink hold talk fruit
people friend

Assignment 54
trap trip train track
trace trunk trick traffic
travel trust trouble trade

Assignment 55
flag flat flock flame
flower flash flesh
floor flood act belong
buy

Assignment 56
cloth clothes clever
clock close class clap
club greedy grapes
grey grocer grumble

Assignment 57
fly sky sty by my sly
shy fry try deny flies
fries tries denies

Assignment 58
baby penny very city
story body jelly rusty
holy lady pony carry
hurry funny army
plenty

Assignment 59
fancy company babies
parties pennies cities
stories carries bodies
money monkey factory

Assignment 60 Revision
traffic trouble clothes
grocer deny tries
penny stories only
money carry

Assignment 61
eat each tea sea east
team clean dream beat
please leave Easter
neat bead leap

Assignment 62
wheat steal heat steam
cheap easy lead mean
season reason speaker
teach weak stream
scream

Assignment 63
dead bread ready
steady instead death
spread threat threaten
already hundred their

Assignment 64
pleasant feather weather
leather wealthy healthy
heather breakfast basket
war warm stuff want

Assignment 65 Revision
each please steal
scream instead spread
once speaker season
dream wealthy warm
weather want

Assignment 66
rails tail nail sail laid
pain hail mail brain
wait plain trail paint

Assignment 67
again afraid play way
say lay May clay pay
tray stay away anyway
faithfully always

Assignment 68
toys joy destroy annoy
convoy half move salt
sugar

Assignment 69
coin soil boil noise
point join voice spoil
joint toilet doing going

Assignment 70 Revision
painting afraid away
faithfully annoy sugar
half toilet destroy salt

Assignment 71
house mouse south
mouth loud cloud our
hour sour shout scout
spout flour

Assignment 72
trousers proud about
pound found round
sound wound ground
bounce fountain
mountain

Assignment 73
now cow sow how
owl fowl howl down
town frown brown
drown crown clown

Assignment 74
crowd prowl flower
tower power shower
brow allow next
picture wind year spend

Assignment 75
grow blow show flow
bow low below fellow
follow yellow own
throw above know
window

Assignment 76 Revision
sour trousers found
about drown crowd
shower picture below
above know hour

Assignment 77
coal load coat boat
goat road soap soak
toad oats foal float
throat

Assignment 78
Paul August Maud
author Autumn cause
because launch applaud
automatic

Assignment 79
saw raw paw lawn
crawl awful talk walk
stalk chalk pepper sore
tore wore

Assignment 80
light night right sight
might sigh high flight
bright fright fight tight
slight height

Assignment 81
eight weight weigh
neigh neighbour freight
straight kind mind
twelve twenty

Assignment 82 Revision
soap throat because
automatic awful lawn
tore bright height
weight neighbour twelve

Assignment 83
herd term germ stern
perch serve several
nerve earth early work
world

Assignment 84
first fir dirty birch firm
skirt thirsty sir thirty
hurt fur burn turn curl

Assignment 85
Thursday Saturday nurse
nursery turkey family
iron heart music shoe
second until build

Assignment 86
dew few new ewe
stew chew drew grew
flew view newspaper
brewery animal cruel
closed present

Assignment 87
age cage wage rage
stage barge hinge fringe
large village postage
carriage courage

Assignment 88
badge bridge edge
hedge smudge ridge
trudge wedge lodger
porridge George quick
quiet quite

Assignment 89 Revision
several early thirsty
nursery shoe build grew
view cruel stage
courage trudge quiet

Assignment 90
air chair hair fair
stairs pair dairy fairy
despair between change
England Wales Scotland
Ireland

Assignment 91
fare dare care mare
hare flare spare scare
shore stare beware
declare welfare

Assignment 92
upstairs scarecrow airman
careful hairdresser
dairymaid staircase danger
Wednesday Tuesday
gentlemen

Assignment 93
field thief chief priest
shield believe piece
niece pie lie tried
cried died whose whole

Assignment 94. Revision
downstairs careful
beware danger believe
piece whose scarecrow
between Ireland

Assignment 95
station   relation
presentation   observation
prevention   invitation
occupation   fraction
correction   direction

Assignment 96
foundation   information
invention   question
examination   education
election   fiction
collection   protection

Assignment 97
explosion   occasion
confusion   pension
admission   discussion
permission   television
colour   country   visit

Assignment 98
cell   face   mice   place
dance   chance   office
since   circle   circus
ounce   saucer   certain

Assignment 99 Revision
occupation   prevention
information   education
invitation   admission
television   country   chance
saucer

Assignment 100
centre   cigarette   exercise
excitement   audience
decide   sincerely   scent
science   scientist

Assignment 101
return   reporter
refreshment   remember
recover   remind   request
double   island   minute
touch   sign

Assignment 102
discover   disgusted
disappear   display
distemper   disappoint
knew   knee   knife   knob
knuckle   knitting
knowledge

Assignment 103
conduct   concert
connection   control
convict   condition
continue   concrete
confess   cough

Assignment 104
nephew   graph
photograph   microphone
telephone   elephant
gramophone   physical
symphony

Assignment 105
wreck   write   wrote
wren   wreath   wrong
wriggle   wringer   quarter
square   cousin   tongue

Assignment 106 Revision
cigarette   sincerely
remember   request   sign
disappoint   knowledge
continue   telephone
nephew   wrong   cousin
pheasant

Assignment 107
really   sorry   couple
interest   machine   break
beauty   reckon   great
happen   hospital   length
course

Assignment 108
busy   business   front
pardon   listen   board
worst   during   travel
probably   error   either
neither   tomorrow   bottle

Assignment 109
idea   hear   near   fear
tear   appear   bear   wear
early   learn

Assignment 110
depend   general
Christmas   dozen
fourteen   fifteen   nineteen
seventeen   eighteen
thirteen   sixteen   motor
eleven

Complete list of titles in the reading scheme

Racing to Read

1 My House/My Garden (24 words)
2 Brenda the Doll/Ruff the Dog/My Mother (12 new words)
3 The Caravan/Mary and Peter (13 new words)
4 In the Garden/Going Camping (14 new words)
5 Tabby the Cat (8 new words)
6 Fire! Fire! (5 new words)
7 In The Park (12 new words)
8 By the River (6 new words)
9 Our Holiday/Lost in the Cave (27 new words)
10 On the Rocks/The Lighthouse (18 new words)
11 Woodside Farm/The Old Watermill (28 new words)
12 At the Zoo/Story Time (33 new words)

Racing to Read Book and Packette or Cassette sets

6 sets including 1 workbook and relevant Racing to Read Book/s.

Racing to Read Second Workbook

For books 3–6.

Early to Read

1 Getting Ready – reading readiness activities
2 Playing in the House
3 Playing in the Garden
4 Working and Playing – workbook
5 Playing in the Park
6 Playing at the Seaside
7 More Working and Playing – workbook

Listening to Sounds

9 Book and Packette Sets – Packette Players are required.
2 Listening to Sounds Workbooks available separately for replacement purposes.
The 9 recordings are also available on 5in tapes at $3\frac{3}{4}$ i.p.s., twin track.

Sound Sense

8 books and 8 extension readers (1a, 1b, 2a, 2b, 3a, 3b, 4a, 4b).